Louise Roques

over

r

Roots

Chapters 25-50

Gladys M. Hunt

13 Discussions for Group Bible Study

Neighborhood Bible Studies Publishers
P.O. Box 222
56 Main Street
Dobbs Ferry, NY 10522
1-800-369-0307
email: nbstudies@aol.com
www.NeighborhoodBibleStudy.org

neighborhood bible studies

GROUP PARTICIPANTS

Name	Address	Phone Number

ISBN 1-880266-31-8
Second Printing 2002
Printed in the United States of America

CONTENTS

HOW TO USE THIS DISCUSSION GUIDE

This study guide uses the inductive approach to Bible study. *It will help you discover for yourself what the Bible says.* It will not give you prepackaged answers. *People remember most what they discover for themselves and what they express in their own words.* The study guide provides three kinds of questions:

1. What does the passage say? What are the facts?
2. What is the meaning of these facts?
3. How does this passage apply to your life?

- Observe the facts carefully before you interpret the meaning of your observations. Then apply the truths you have discovered to life today. Resist the temptation to skip the fact questions since we are not as observant as we think. Find the facts quickly so you can spend more time on their meaning and application.

- *The purpose of Bible study is not just to know more Bible truths but to apply them.* Allow these truths to make a difference in how you think and act, in your attitudes and relationships, in the quality and direction of your life.

- Each discussion requires about one hour. Decide on the amount of time to add for socializing and prayer.

- *Share the leadership.* If a different person is the moderator or question-asker each week, interest grows and members feel the group belongs to everyone. The Bible is the authority in the group, not the question-asker.

- When a group grows to more than ten, the quiet people become quieter. Plan to grow and multiply. You can meet as two groups in the same house or begin another group so that more people can participate and benefit.

TOOLS FOR AN EFFECTIVE BIBLE STUDY

1. A study guide for each person in the group.

2. A modern translation of the Bible such as:
   NEW INTERNATIONAL VERSION (NIV)
   CONTEMPORARY ENGLISH VERSION (CEV)
   JERUSALEM BIBLE (JB)
   NEW AMERICAN STANDARD BIBLE (NASB)
   REVISED ENGLISH BIBLE (REB)
   NEW REVISED STANDARD VERSION (NRSV)

3. An English dictionary.

4. A map of the Lands of the Bible in a Bible or in the study guide.

5. Your conviction that the Bible is worth studying.

GUIDELINES FOR AN EFFECTIVE STUDY

1. Stick to the passage under discussion.

2. Avoid tangents. If the subject is not addressed in the passage, put it on hold until after the study.

3. Let the Bible speak for itself. Do not quote other authorities or rewrite it to say what you want it to say.

4. Apply the passage personally and honestly.

5. Listen to one another to sharpen your insights.

6. Prepare by reading the Bible passage and thinking through the questions during the week.

7. Begin and end on time.

HELPS FOR THE QUESTION-ASKER

1. Prepare by reading the passage several times, using different translations if possible. Ask for God's help in understanding it. Consider how the questions might be answered. Observe which questions can be answered quickly and which may require more time.

2. Begin on time.

3. Lead the group in opening prayer or ask someone ahead of time to do so. Don't take anyone by surprise.

4. Ask for a different volunteer to read each Bible section. Read the question. Wait for an answer. Rephrase the question if necessary. Resist the temptation to answer the question yourself. Move to the next question. Skip questions already answered by the discussion.

5. Encourage everyone to participate. Ask the group, "What do the rest of you think?" "What else could be added?"

6. Receive all answers warmly. If needed, ask, "In which verse did you find that?" "How does that fit with verse...?"

7. If a tangent arises, ask, "Do we find the answer to that here?" Or suggest, "Let's write that down and look for the information as we go along."

8. Discourage members who are too talkative by saying, "When I read the next question, let's hear from someone who hasn't spoken yet today."

9. Use the summary questions to bring the study to a conclusion on time.

10. Close the study with prayer.

11. Decide on one person to be the host and another person to ask the questions at the next discussion.

INTRODUCTION

Genesis, *Book 2, Chapters 25-50,* is the continued story of God putting into action his plan to save his people. While it seems to be Jacob's story, it is in fact God's story.

The story began in particular when God took the initiative and intervened in the life of one man, Abraham. God's purpose in calling Abraham to himself was to bless him. He gave Abraham far-reaching promises of descendants as numerous as the stars in the heavens and a land that would belong to these people. That the story begins on a small scale is obvious when Abraham dies, leaving one promised son, Isaac. But God promised even more than that. ***I will be with you and be your God.***

The first study in this section of *Genesis* begins with the death of Abraham. Isaac inherits God's promise. Like his father, Isaac must wait some time before his wife conceives and bears two sons, Jacob and Esau, whose struggles dramatize the continued story of God's blessing and choosing.

The remainder of the *Genesis* account is the story of Jacob's family. It is the story of God working out the fulfillment of his great plan for the world. The people in the story have no special talents to make them worthy of God's blessing. Their lives are laced with humanity's fear, deceit, and waywardness. The marvel is the way God works through all their life events to display his grace and purposefulness.

God's grace does not leave these characters alone; he gives them awesome experiences, experiences which help them trust him. Though he lets them wander, he is with them. God is patient, but he pursues his purposes. In the end, Jacob finds himself, and his many descendants, not in the land God promised but in Egypt, a refugee from the famine in Canaan. But the *God of his fathers Abraham and Isaac* (Genesis 48:15, 21) is more real to him than ever before and he is strong in his confidence that God will bring them back home.

In this story of grace, Joseph is a stellar player. Taunted, sold as a slave, believed dead by his father, this son is the one who teaches the family what it means to forgive, and ends up saving the life of his family for God's future purposes for them.

Genesis, Chapters 25-50, is a drama of frail human beings and a great God. The life of Jacob demonstrates how God can change a person, dealing with all the twists in his nature. The life of Joseph shows God's saving sovereignty that not only overcomes wrong deeds but ends with salvation. In many ways these chapters in *Genesis* are the gospel in the Old Testament.

DISCUSSION 1

Twin Sons for Isaac and Rebekah

GENESIS 25:19-34; PSALM 94:8-15

Abraham, chosen by God to be the father of God's own people, died full of good years. He left one son, Isaac, as heir to the promise that this family would become too many to number. One son was a meager beginning for the expansive promises of God. This study hurries on to tell us of the birth of two sons to Isaac to assure us that God's plan is operative. The story also reminds us that God's timing is not always our timing, but that he controls affairs even when they look out of control.

1. What two choices do you have when life doesn't go the way you expected?

READ GENESIS 25:19-34

2. Compare the marriage blessing given Rebekah by her family in Genesis 24:60 with the realities of her life in Genesis 25:21.

How long have Rebekah and Isaac waited for the birth of a child? Compare verse 20 with 26b.

3. Why might the phrase ***Isaac prayed for his wife*** be an understatement?

4. What specific promises had God given to Abraham about his family (Genesis 12:2-5 and 15:4, 5)?

5. The LORD's promise of offspring first made when Abraham was 75 years old was not fulfilled until he was 100 and Sarah was 90.

   Why do you think God made Abraham and Sarah wait so long for fulfillment of the promises?

   What does this tell you about the attitude God wants his children to have toward him?

6. Why is *waiting* so difficult?

7. What have you learned from waiting for God to answer your prayers?

8. After the LORD answers Isaac's prayer, what troubles Rebekah (verses 22, 23)?

   What dramatic information is Rebekah given about what to expect?

9. Compare the character traits of Jacob and Esau (verses 25-34).

Note: The birthright was the privilege of the firstborn. It meant headship of the family and a larger share in the estate, as well as special status and blessing. It could be transferred only by a binding oath.

10. The last words in this chapter might have read, ***So Jacob took advantage of his brother***. Instead, what does the ending tell you about Esau's view of his birthright? (See Hebrews 12:16, 17 for the New Testament's comment on Esau.)

11. Esau is irreverent in his appreciation of his heritage; Jacob is grasping. What contemporary examples of these same faults can you give?

In what ways do temptations to these attitudes come to you?

READ PSALM 94:8-15

12. How does the LORD deal with people who do stupid things?

13. What assurance does the psalmist have about God's discipline (verse 14)?

14. What comfort does God's personal involvement in your life give you?

Summary

1. What benefits are there to being confined to God's ways and his timetable for you?

2. What have you learned about human choices and God's grace in this study?

Prayer

Lord, we are so often in a hurry. We want to see the beginning and the happy ending right now. We are so often like Esau, wanting to solve our hunger problems our way. Protect us from our own destructive choices. Thank you for teaching us that you have long-range purposes in what you do and what you allow. Teach us more about the practical ways in which we need to learn to trust you. For our good and your glory. Amen.

DISCUSSION 2

Fear and Faith

GENESIS 26; PSALM 25:8-15

It is likely that the events of this study precede the birth of Esau and Jacob. Commentator Derek Kidner, writing about the placement of this chapter, says that after Abraham's death in Genesis 25, "the story hastens on to the new generation before pausing for Isaac himself, whose affairs can wait until the next chapter: such is the importance of succession."**

Genesis 26 is the only chapter given entirely to Isaac. He is not the pioneer his father Abraham was. He is primarily a consolidator, a bridge between the spectacular events of Abraham's life and God's dealings with Jacob. The famine incident in this study may well be Isaac's most unsettling adventure away from home. His job was to pass on to his sons all that God had revealed about the family's destiny and God's faithfulness.

READ GENESIS 26:1-11

1. What mixture of fear and faith do you see in verses 1-11?

2. Why are these two attitudes incompatible companions?

**Derek Kidner, *The Tyndale Old Testament Commentary: Genesis* (Downers Grove, IL: InterVarsity Press, 1967) p. 150.

What inevitably results when fear and faith are in conflict?

3. How does God encourage Isaac at this unsettling time of famine?

Note: *When food was scarce the choice was to head either for Egypt, irrigated by the Nile, or the coast of Canaan with its higher rainfall. Isaac opted for the nearer place and God approved.*

4. What effect do the promises of God in verses 3-5 have on Isaac's fears of verse 7?

   What example from your own life mirrors this same conflict between faith and fear?

5. How might Isaac have jeopardized the family line by his deceit? Compare with Genesis 12:10-20.

6. How does the Philistine King Abimelech put to shame Isaac's devious behavior?

   How serious a matter is this to Abimelech (verse 11)?

Note: ***When Isaac had been there a long time*** *(verse 8) indicates that Isaac's fears have been groundless.*

READ GENESIS 26:12-35

7. How does Isaac fare in Gerar? Why?

At what point does Isaac overstay his welcome?

8. What situations in history come to your mind in which people have been displaced because of envy? In your own life?

9. How does Hebrews 11:9, 10 link Isaac to his father Abraham's faith and obedience?

10. After the difficulties over the wells in Gerar, how does Isaac's experience in Beersheba both comfort and reward him (verses 23-25)?

What three actions does Isaac take in verse 25, and what is their significance?

How do they give some permanence to his life?

11. Compare 26:28, 29 with 21:22-31. What good sense do Abimelech and his men show in these passages?

Note: Abimelech and Phicol may be official names or recurring family names.

12. How does Isaac display both conciliation and assertiveness in his treatment of Abimelech and his men?

Note: Verses 34 and 35 seem out of place here. Remember their implications when you study the next chapter of Genesis.

READ PSALM 25:8-15

13. According to the psalmist, what does God do for people like Isaac who ***fear the LORD***? List the verbs.

14. On what basis can you, and Isaac, ask forgiveness (verse 11)?

15. Express the meaning of verse 15 in your own words.

SUMMARY

1. What do you think Isaac learned about the LORD from his experiences in Gerar?

2. What can you learn from Isaac's response to the LORD in Beersheba?

Prayer

Lord, how foolish our fears look when we read of your faithfulness. Help us to learn to trust you and to keep our focus on you. Thank you for taking the responsibility to instruct us, to guide us, and to teach us your ways. We thank you that you never waste any of our experiences. May we simplify our lives by our obedience to you. For your glory and our good. Amen.

DISCUSSION 3

The Blessing

GENESIS 27,28; PSALM 46

Don't be too hard on the people in this study; you will find they are like people you know, even yourself. Reader sympathy generally goes to Esau, twice robbed by an aggressive brother. However, each character in this story is responsible for personal actions. No excuses are allowed. The other side of the story involves God's sovereignty, a reality human beings are prone to forget. God is not confounded by human error; he keeps to his original plan to make a mighty people out of Abraham's seed.

READ GENESIS 27

1. In planning to give Esau the birthright blessing (27:4), what word from the LORD does Isaac ignore (25:21-26)?

2. What oath does Esau break by agreeing to his father's plan to give him the blessing (25:31-34)?

Note: The blessing ceremony was not meant to be a secret event, but a family affair to celebrate. Isaac was not as near death as he thought (verse 2). He lived at least 20 more years (Genesis 35:27-29).

3. Why do you think Rebekah acts as she does in light of God's words to her in Genesis 25:23?

How is she prepared to deal with the consequences if her strategy fails?

4. Why would Isaac ignore his doubts and let himself be so easily fooled by Jacob?

5. How does Jacob further involve himself in deception in his answers to Isaac's questions?

6. At what point does Esau recognize the seriousness of selling his birthright?

7. How are each of the four characters in this story at fault?

8. What do you learn about the consequences of human choices?

9. With which of these four characters do you most identify? Why?

   How does fear about the possible outcome of an event influence your ability to trust God in facing it?

10. Rebekah loses Jacob in order to save him. What reason does she give Isaac to send Jacob away (verse 46)?

Note: Rebekah does not live to see Jacob again.

READ GENESIS 28

11. As he sends Jacob away to Rebekah's family to find a wife, how does Isaac reinforce and expand the blessing upon Jacob? (Compare 28:3, 4 and 27:27-29).

12. Picture yourself as Jacob, an accomplice to his mother's plot, leaving the home he loves, afraid and alone as night falls. What do you learn about God from the encounter in verses 12-15?

Who takes the initiative in this encounter?

Note: This is no minor occasion: ***There above it stood the LORD.*** *God deals in person with Jacob. The angels play the role of arresting Jacob's attention.*

13. How does the message God gives Jacob fit his circumstances?

What meaning does it give his life?

14. How does Jacob respond to the events of his life?

How does Jacob respond to God's intervention in his life (verse 20)?

15. Think in terms of *unworthiness, guilt, needing grace, needing purpose.* In what ways has your own experience with God been like Jacob's?

READ PSALM 46

16. What fear-causing events are mentioned in this psalm?

17. What truths comfort the psalmist?

18. How can you have the same comfort in the face of fear that the psalmist had (verse 10)?

SUMMARY

1. In what ways does God's encounter with Jacob in 28:13-15 expose the utter foolishness of a son conniving with his mother against his father?

2. How would the lives of the people in this story have been different if they had fully trusted God to work for their good?

PRAYER

Lord, we so often let life and its problems push us into taking charge in ways that deny our faith in you. Forgive us for our resemblance to the people in today's study. Help us to cultivate the habit of quietness before you. Teach us how to wait for you, to listen and to obey. Above all, help us to heed the instruction to **Be still and know that I am God.** *For your glory and our good. Amen.*

DISCUSSION 4

Jacob and Laban

GENESIS 29; 30:1-24; PSALM 42

When Jacob arrives in Haran he meets his match in his uncle Laban who is as much an opportunist as Jacob. Laban is quick to realize that Jacob has arrived in Haran in a vulnerable position. While seeming to be the supportive uncle, he takes advantage of Jacob as Jacob has taken advantage of Esau. In this study we see this rule of life in action: what you sow, you also reap.

READ GENESIS 29

1. How does Jacob show his enterprising nature as he arrives in Haran (verses 1-10)?

2. Why isn't Jacob in a hurry to return home?

3. What do you learn from Jacob's situation about the way wrong choices can complicate your life?

4. Isaac has not provided Jacob a bride price as Abraham did to obtain a bride for Isaac (Genesis 24:10, 22). Since Jacob loves Rachel, how does he intend to solve this problem of bride-price?

Note: Rachel is probably a young adolescent, maybe even a pre-teen, at this time. Seven years service for a wife may well be an accepted period that would represent the normal bride-price and assure Laban that Jacob's intentions were serious.

5. How does Jacob the deceiver respond to Laban's trickery?

6. How would you describe Laban's character from his actions in 24:29-31, 50, 51; 29:15, 19, 25-27?

7. What new insights do you get into Jacob from his willingness to work hard?

Note: The whole wedding affair is of another culture. It is male dominated. The father feels free to market his daughters any way he wants to. No mention is made of Rachel's feelings or how they kept her quiet when she found she was not going to be the bride, nor of Leah's self-esteem in all of this.

8. How is God's mercy for Leah revealed (verses 31-35)?

9. When you have experienced rejection, in what ways has God shown his mercy to you?

10. What do the names of Leah's first three sons reveal about the domestic tensions she lives with every day?

11. What is significant about the birth of Leah's fourth son?

Note: The unloved Leah becomes the wife who bears the son from whose lineage the Messiah would come. **Out of the tribe of Judah...** *(Psalm 78:68 and Revelation 5:5)*

READ GENESIS 30:1-24

12. From this passage, what words would you use to describe Jacob's household?

What human needs are being exposed in this story?

13. What is Jacob's part in sowing the seeds of bitterness (29:30-34; 30:1, 2, 19, 20)?

14. Even though their motives are flawed, how does God respond to the desperate prayers of Leah and Rachel?

What do you learn from this about your own prayers and the grace of God?

READ PSALM 42

15. What conflict is honestly faced in this psalm?

16. What options do you have when life doesn't go the way you want it to go?

Summary

1. What consequences does Jacob suffer as a result of his behavior toward his brother and father?

2. What long-range problems do deceit and envy bring to families?

3. What truths about God do you learn from this study?

Prayer

Lord, we see Jacob and Laban as deceivers, and we don't like what we see. But we know our own hearts, and confess to you that we are deceivers also. We pretend to truth we do not live. We know we have reacted spitefully in envy in family affairs. O God, forgive us. Thank you that you see through all the masks we wear and the good that we pretend. You see our hearts. You know that we often cry out to you in impatience and fear, and we forget that you are good and unfailing in your love toward us. Make us genuine on the inside and on the outside. For our good and your glory. Amen.

DISCUSSION 5

Jacob's Flight

GENESIS 30:25-43; 31; PSALM 13

Jacob has been in Haran twenty years. For twenty years he worked hard for Laban, all the time planning and scheming to improve his own position in life. While Laban is away shearing his sheep, Jacob decides the time has come to leave Haran. He gives his large, slow-moving company a three-day head start toward Canaan. He hardly hopes to escape completely, but he manages to cross the Euphrates before Laban overtakes him. Jacob's subsequent encounter with Laban is only one of three important meetings on his way home.

READ GENESIS 30:25-43

1. After over fourteen years of service for Laban, Jacob feels it is time to leave Haran. What does he ask Laban to give him (verses 25, 26)?

2. Why is Laban reluctant to let Jacob go?

3. What plan does each man make to outwit the other?

Note: It was thought that white patches before the ewe's eyes would cause white-flecked animals.

READ GENESIS 31:1-21

4. What does Jacob's success cost him?

5. No record is given of God speaking to Jacob for twenty years. Why does God speak now and what does he say (verses 3, 11-13)?

6. How does God speak to you today, and how do you recognize his voice?

7. What complaints do the daughters have against their father Laban?

8. By sneaking away like a coward while Laban is gone, what life-lesson has Jacob not yet learned (verse 3)?

9. What lessons have you learned when you have made a choice to trust God instead of taking charge yourself?

READ GENESIS 31:22-55

10. Why does Laban go after Jacob with such fervor?

What is his intent?

How does God graciously intervene to save both of these men (verse 24)?

11. What are Laban's accusations against Jacob when they finally come face to face?

Note: Why did Rachel steal the household gods? At the very least, they were valuable, and she may have thought them her due, verse 15. Nuzi tablets indicate that possession of these gods strengthened a claim to an inheritance, which may account for Laban's eagerness for an oath that forbade future raiding.

12. How does each of these men try to out do the other in manipulating the situation to his advantage (verses 26-30 and 38-42)?

13. Knowing he is defeated, how does Laban make the best of the situation?

14. What is the purpose of the piled up stones and the oath Jacob and Laban take (verses 44-54)?

15. Why is open dealing always better than scheming in handling difficult relationships?

16. How do the psalmist's complaints against God (verses 1, 2) relate to Jacob's life?

17. How real is the conflict between fear and faith in your own life?

SUMMARY

1. What growth in faith in God do you see in Jacob and Laban as this study ends?

2. How have difficult relationships helped you to grow in faith?

PRAYER

Lord, it is easy to discuss the way Jacob and Laban take matters into their own hands by plotting and manipulating situations to their own advantage. It is harder to see when we do this ourselves. Teach us how foolish this is. Help us to handle our relationships openly and honestly. Give us a growing faith that believes you when you say, "I will be with you." For your glory and our good. Amen.

DISCUSSION 6

Jacob Meets Esau

GENESIS 32, 33; PSALM 18:1-6

Jacob survived his first crisis in the confrontation with Laban, but he is not a free man. His past still haunts him. He must face his brother, Esau, or he will never feel safe in his own land. Jacob sends messengers to find Esau in Seir, located in the land of Edom south of the Dead Sea. He appeals to Esau, hoping to "find favor in his sight." To his surprise Esau takes an initiative of his own; he comes in person to meet Jacob. But Jacob has an even more important meeting before he can get right with Esau: his meeting with God.

READ GENESIS 32:1-21

1. Facing this new and more terrible threat of dealing with Esau, what encouragement does Jacob receive from God in verses 1 and 2?

2. Having taken the initiative in contacting Esau (verses 3-5), what is Jacob's response when he hears of Esau's approach with 400 men?

3. Read again Jacob's prayer in verses 9-12. Of what does he remind God (verses 9, 12)?

What does he confess to God (verses 10, 11)?

What does he ask of God (verse 11)?

4. Why is this a good model for your own prayers?

5. Jacob is still Jacob. What is his strategy in dealing with Esau?

6. What does Jacob hope to accomplish by sending a sizeable gift on ahead to Esau (verse 20)?

READ GENESIS 32:22-32

7. What conflicts within Jacob are brought to a head by his wrestling with God at Peniel?

8. Why are the crippling, the naming and the blessing necessary for Jacob if he is to fulfill the role God has for him?

9. How has this encounter made Jacob both stronger and weaker?

10. What do you learn about God's long-range purposes and grace in your own life from Jacob's encounter with God?

Read Genesis 33

11. What favoritism does Jacob show as he organizes his family in preparation for meeting Esau?

12. What has happened to the enmity between Esau and Jacob?

What initiative does each brother take?

13. Why does Jacob press his gift upon Esau (verse 10) and by taking the gift, what does Esau affirm?

14. What experience have you had of this kind of reconciliation?

Why does genuine reconciliation always have the touch of God on it?

15. In refusing Esau's offers, what does Jacob imply he will do (verses 12, 15)?

What is his real intent (verse 17)?

16. From your own experience, how are such patterns of behavior hard to change, even though you have met God as Jacob did?

Note: Jacob's instructions from God were to go home, which meant Bethel. Seir is some distance out of Jacob's way and would distract Jacob from his instructions to go home. We can only guess why Jacob didn't simply tell this to Esau.

PSALM 18:1-6

17. What desperate feelings does the psalm-writer describe in verses 4, 5 that Jacob might have claimed for his own as he thought of facing Esau?

18. Saved from his enemies, the psalm-writer uses strong words to describe the LORD (verses 1, 2). Which of these descriptions would you use to tell how God has helped you?

SUMMARY

1. Why does reconciliation sometimes depend on more than explanations or words?

2. When Jacob builds an altar in his own country, the name he gives it means *the God of Israel,* or *mighty is the God of Israel* (33:20). How does this relate to his wrestling with God at Peniel, (32:22-31)?

PRAYER

Lord God of Abraham, Isaac and Jacob, we are amazed at your grace in intervening in the lives of those you call to yourself. Jacob didn't deserve all the favor you showed him. We do not deserve the favor you show us. Thank you for wrestling with us in our inner debates about whether we will let you be LORD *in our lives. Lord, we pray that you will not let us get away from you. By your grace, take charge of our hearts. For your glory and our good. Amen.*

DISCUSSION 7

Going to Bethel the Hard Way

GENESIS 34—36; PSALM 121

God has told Jacob to go home. Instead, Jacob stops a day's journey short of Bethel. Bethel stands for everything that matters spiritually. Shechem, a trading crossroads within the borders of Canaan, stands for economic advantage. Jacob forgets his call to be a pilgrim when he buys a piece of land and settles into life in Shechem. Even though he builds an altar and claims his new name, calling God the God of Israel, he is not where God has told him to go. As Lot did, Jacob has chosen his site for the wrong reasons. This study reveals the cost of his disobedience and the trouble it brings. Only fear for his life makes Jacob hear again God's call to Bethel.

READ GENESIS 34

1. A terrible assault has taken place. What is Shechem and Hamor's solution to what happened?

2. What does Hamor's offer during the family conference with Jacob and Dinah's brothers, imply about his hopes for the future union of these Canaanites and the children of Israel (verses 9, 10, 16)?

3. Why do the innocent members of the Shechem community agree to the plan to be circumcised (verses 21-23)?

4. What outcome does the deceit of Dinah's brothers and their subsequent violence bring to this tragedy?

5. How does this massacre jeopardize the future of the children of Israel?

6. From your own experience, what results always follow the enticement to get revenge?

READ GENESIS 35

7. What memories is God evoking for Jacob in the instructions he gives in verse 1?

8. What indicates that Jacob's family has been in Shechem long enough to become contaminated by its culture (verse 2, 4)?

9. Today what gods do people collect, perhaps unaware of how they keep them from hearing God's voice?

10. What witness does Jacob give his family members (verse 3)?

Some people think of faith as a private matter. Why is it necessary to speak about what you believe to your family?

11. How does Jacob's large company of people manage to escape without being attacked by surrounding tribes (verse 5)?

Note: Verse 8 tells us that the company passed by the grave site of Rebekah's nurse, who came with Rebekah (24:59) when she was betrothed to Isaac. It is assumed that she died earlier. There is no indication that she was with Jacob's company. Some commentators believe that the mention of Deborah pays oblique tribute to Rebekah, who probably is no longer living.

12. When God appears again at Bethel (verses 9-12) what does Jacob learn about himself?

about his future?

Compare this message with the original Bethel encounter in 28:13-15.

13. What does God reveal about himself that assures the fulfillment of what is promised?

14. What family events bring grief to Jacob as he travels home?

Note: Reuben's indecent behavior toward Bilhah is mentioned only in passing, but it affects firstborn Reuben who in 49:4 has lost his birthright.

15. The homecoming is tersely summarized: ***Jacob came home to his father Isaac in Mamre*** (verses 27-29). What insights into a biblical view of death do you get from the phrase ***he was gathered to his people*** (verse 29)?

QUICKLY SCAN GENESIS 36

16. Although Esau does not receive the birthright, how does his clan fare?

Note: Esau's family moved to the inhospitable land that Isaac predicted in 27:39. When one phase of a story is completed in Genesis, the pattern is to give the family genealogy. Chapter 36 records the people who came from Esau's lineage. The rest of Genesis will now pick up the main thread, and focus on the sons of Jacob.

PSALM 121

17. In what sense does this psalm prove true for Jacob, regardless of whether he deserves this kind of help?

18. What does it mean to you that ***the Maker of heaven and earth*** watches over your life in this way?

SUMMARY

1. What does Jacob learn from his experience in Shechem?

2. To what lengths does God go in this study to fulfill his purposes for Jacob?

How does God's work in Jacob's life both warn and encourage you in your spiritual journey?

PRAYER

Father God, we are amazed and encouraged by your patience. Thank you that you don't waste our mistakes, even though they bear sad consequences. Thank you that you have a long-range plan for us as we trust you, and that you have both power and the goodness to bring it about for your glory and our good.

(in unison) ***The Lord will watch over your coming and going both now and forevermore. Amen.***

DISCUSSION 8

Jacob's Family Affairs

GENESIS 37, 38; PSALM 36

The folly and wickedness that plague the human race is condensed in this story of Jacob's family. Envy, pride, arrogance, we find them all in this study. Full of suspense, it is also full of warning and revelation of the grace of God.

Chapter 38 seems a rude interruption as Joseph's future hangs in the balance, but it is a piece of family history that settles the seniority within the family line. Reuben has disqualified himself as the first son when he takes his father's concubine; Simeon and Levi caused the massacre at Shechem. Judah, the fourth son of Leah, becomes the front runner in the family line. Who will be Judah's heir? Chapter 38 answers that question, and it has consequences in the large scheme of history.

READ GENESIS 37

1. How do Jacob's actions fuel the flames of jealousy in Joseph's older brothers (verses 3, 13)?

2. What should Jacob have learned from his own childhood (25:28)?

Why do you think people often exhibit the same behaviors in their own family life that they resented in their childhood?

3. How do Joseph's rather naive actions cause the pot of jealousy to boil over (verses 2, 5, 8, 11)?

4. How do the brothers' differing ideas of how to get rid of Joseph end up saving his life?

5. Whose idea is it to sell Joseph as a slave?

6. How is a goat once again used in deception (27:9; 37:31, 32)?

7. Whose position is worse: young Joseph in terror at being taken away as a slave, or that of the brothers who must live with their grieving father? Why?

In what situations have you found a guilty conscience uncomfortable?

READ CHAPTER 38

8. Why does Judah fail to give his third son to marry Tamar, the widow of his first son Er?

Note: It was a widespread custom, known as levirate marriage, that the brothers of a deceased man should marry his widow and thus produce an heir for the dead man. The family was responsible to ensure a continuity of the lineage of the dead relative.

9. What is Tamar's strategy to become the matriarch of Judah's family?

10. To his credit, how does Judah evaluate Tamar's actions in comparison with his own?

Note: The double standard for sexual behavior for men and women led the prophets to cry out against this hypocrisy (Hosea 4:14).

11. What does this unusual story tell you about the sharp moral decline within the chosen family?

12. Perez, the firstborn of Tamar's twins, is listed as an ancestor of David (Ruth 4:18) and in the genealogy of Christ in Matthew 1:3. In what ways is your understanding of the amazing grace of God growing through these studies?

PSALM 36

13. What is the sinfulness of the wicked (verses 1–4)?

14. In contrast, what four attributes does the psalmist give the LORD (verses 5, 6)?

15. What safety is offered those who trust in the LORD (verses 7-9)?

16. How is the statement ***In your light we see light.*** (verse 9b) true in your life?

SUMMARY

1. What sinful patterns of living are obvious both in Joseph's story and that of Judah and Tamar?

How does God's control over human history evidence itself in these two stories?

PRAYER

Lord, jealousy and arrogance produce trouble that lingers a long time. We ask you to take from our hearts the anger and pride that lead to spiteful living. Help us to face up to conflicts and wrongdoings with your standards of truth and justice. Give us the grace to show to others the same loving concern that you show to us. For your glory and our good. Amen.

DISCUSSION 9

Joseph, a Man of Integrity

GENESIS 39, 40; PSALM 71:1-8

Joseph's prospects looked bleak indeed: kidnapped by his brothers while still a teenager, then sold as a slave to traveling Midianites who in turn sold him to an Egyptian official. Injustice seems to dog his steps. One might expect that the deep pain and isolation in his childhood would warp his personality and lead to a life full of resentment and fear. Here is a victim, if ever there was one! But that is not the Joseph we meet in this study. He is a resilient, resourceful, attractive young man in contact with God. At the time of this study he has probably been in Potiphar's service about ten years.

READ GENESIS 39

1. What evidences do you see in this chapter that God is blessing Joseph?

2. How is Joseph's conduct in sharp contrast to Judah's actions in chapter 38?

3. How might Joseph use his freedom from supervision and his privileged position to rationalize his involvement with Mrs. Potiphar, especially in light of verse 10?

4. How does seeing Mrs. Potiphar's proposition as an offense against her husband and against God help Joseph do what is right (verse 9)?

In a culture laced with psychological explanations, how are you tempted to rationalize sin rather than call it by its right name?

5. How does Joseph handle the final ambush (verse 12)?

How does Mrs. Potiphar handle the rejection?

6. What recourse does Joseph have concerning the injustice he suffers in Potiphar's house?

7. For the second time, Joseph is a victim of someone's spite. How might he have reacted to such a humiliating event?

What makes his life bearable?

8. What do you do when you are treated spitefully or unjustly?

9. Which situation offers the most satisfaction: clandestine encounters with Potiphar's wife or prison life with the LORD'S presence and favor?

10. Who likely is the captain of the guard who places the baker and the cupbearer under Joseph's care in the king's prison (39:1 and 40:3)?

What insights does this give you about Potiphar's evaluation of Joseph's character?

Note: Joseph could have been executed for an assault on Potiphar's wife. Instead he was placed in the king's prison which may indicate that Potiphar had misgivings in punishing Joseph, but could hardly ignore his wife's accusations.

11. What attitude of concern does Joseph show toward these two prisoners he attends?

12. Why is Joseph confident that he can interpret the dreams of these two men?

What do you notice about his courage in doing so?

13. Why does Joseph plead his own case before Pharaoh's chief cupbearer (verses 14, 15)?

14. When events turn out as dramatically as Joseph predicts, *how* could the cupbearer forget to mention Joseph?

What illustration from your own life demonstrates this kind of forgetfulness?

PSALM 71:1-8

15. In what ways is the experience of the psalmist like that of Joseph?

16. What truths undergird the person who feels despair?

17. How have you found that knowing God changes your point of view about life and its bitter disappointments?

SUMMARY

1. Where do you see the hand of God in this study even in the face of self-centered forgetfulness and disregard of Joseph on the part of others?

2. What character traits has God built into Joseph?

PRAYER

Lord, this study touches our own lives. We want to ask, Why do bad things happen to good people? Remind us of your sovereignty over our lives, and help us to remember that the story is not all told yet. Give us courage from Joseph's example. Be our Rock and our Fortress in difficult times. Rescue us from our fears. Help us to trust you, for our good and your glory. Amen.

DISCUSSION 10

Joseph, Delivered and Deliverer

GENESIS 41, 42; PSALM 105:7-22

Joseph's darkest moment must have come when he realizes that the one man who could help him get out of prison has forgotten all about him. Two years is a long time to wait, but Joseph's subsequent life shows no sign of bitterness. He seems to make the most of his lot. When the time comes for him to appear before Pharaoh Joseph has not forgotten God.

When the famine that Joseph predicted and planned for reaches its height, it has been twenty years since his brothers sold him into bondage. Let your imagination capture the drama and the pathos of Joseph's position in being the deliverer of the children of Israel.

READ GENESIS 41

1. What circumstances lead the butler to suddenly remember Joseph?

2. Why is this a far more auspicious time and way than if the butler had remembered Joseph two years earlier?

How might Pharaoh have viewed Joseph two years earlier and how does he view him now?

3. What has "waiting for God" taught you about the wisdom of his timing in your own life?

4. How does Joseph set Pharaoh straight about his ability to interpret dreams (verses 16, 25, 28, 32)?

What does Pharaoh conclude after listening to Joseph (verses 38, 39)?

5. What changes do you observe in Joseph from the boy who told his brothers about his dreams?

6. How does Pharaoh respond to Joseph's proposals?

7. How has Joseph been prepared in Potiphar's service for his new responsibilities?

In what ways has Joseph's faith been publicly vindicated?

8. What details in Joseph's life change drastically between chapter 40 and the end of chapter 41?

9. What do the names Joseph gives his sons (41:51, 52) indicate about his attitude toward the past?

READ GENESIS 42

10. When the famine drives his brothers to come to Egypt, why does Joseph appear to deal harshly with them?

How do the interviews affect both his brothers and Joseph?

11. What is the point of the three days in prison and keeping one brother as hostage?

12. Why are the brothers afraid when Joseph gives them more than they ask for?

Why do people often think that unaccountable things in life are punishment from God?

13. What do you learn about the brothers' love for Jacob from the interaction in verses 29-38?

READ PSALM 105:7-22

14. What evidences do you find in this psalm that the LORD has a plan which he is carrying out for the sake of his people?

SUMMARY

1. What has waiting for God produced in Joseph's life?

2. What does the famine do in Jacob's family life?

3. What have you learned from this study that will help you to trust God more?

PRAYER

Heavenly Father, thank you that there are no circumstances in our lives that catch you unaware. When we sit imprisoned by our fears and sorrows, you are with us, ready in your time to deliver us for a greater good than we could dream of. Teach us, Lord, how to wait for you to complete your purposes. Thank you that you were mindful of Joseph, but thank you, too, that you don't write off people like Joseph's brothers. Take our lives and discipline us for the good you have for us. For your glory and our good. Amen.

DISCUSSION 11

Joseph: Forgiveness

GENESIS 43—45; PSALM 31:19-24

The continuing famine brings desperate hunger. Nearly two years have passed since Jacob's sons made their first trip to Egypt. Poor Simeon! Jacob has to face the facts, and his sons must face Joseph in Egypt once more. They have no other choice but to turn to Egypt for help.

READ GENESIS 43

1. How is fearful Jacob persuaded to change his mind and allow Benjamin to accompany the brothers to get food?

2. When the brothers arrive in Egypt, what especially mystifies them (verse 23 and 33)?

3. Use your imagination. What do you think the brothers talk about when Simeon is brought out to them?

4. What do you think is happening inside of Joseph as he entertains his brothers during this visit?

Read Genesis 44

5. Why is Joseph continuing to test his brothers (44:1-5?)

6. What causes the brothers to make so rash a promise in verse 9 that the steward himself immediately amends it?

7. How have the brothers, especially Judah, changed since the events of 37:25-28?

Read Genesis 45

8. Why does Judah's appeal (44:18-34) especially touch Joseph's heart?

9. Why might Joseph's brothers be reluctant to ***come close*** (verse 4)?

10. How does Joseph's view of God affect his perspective on all that happened to him (verses 5, 7, 8, 9)?

In what ways have you found your view of God the key to interpreting what happens in your life?

11. Why is Joseph able to show mercy to his brothers?

What experience have the brothers had of grace and forgiveness?

What is necessary for you to be able to show mercy to people who have wronged you?

12. What grand plan does Joseph put into action, and why does he do this?

13. How do you evaluate Joseph's reputation from Pharaoh's response to the news that Joseph has found his family?

14. Why is Joseph's revelation of himself both good news and bad news to the brothers?

From your own personal experience, why is it sometimes hard to accept mercy and forgiveness for what you have done?

15. Why do you think Joseph gives his stunned brothers the warning in verse 24?

About what do you think the brothers might be tempted to argue on the way home?

16. How does the return of his sons and the news they bring change the self-absorbed, negative attitude old Jacob has shown?

PSALM 31:19-24

17. If Jacob had access to this psalm, what ideas would cause him to say "Amen"?

18. What ideas from this psalm make you want to say "Amen"?

SUMMARY

1. Contrast who Joseph believed was in charge of affairs with who his frightened brothers thought was in charge.

2. How did the difference affect their freedom to do what is right?

PRAYER

Lord God, thank you for this exciting, historical account of grace and forgiveness. How freeing forgiveness is! Help us to let go of resentments and wrongs that need forgiveness. Give us a faith like Joseph's that sees your hand in every circumstance. For your glory and our good. Amen.

DISCUSSION 12

Israel Goes to Egypt

GENESIS 46, 47; PSALM 28:6-9

The uncertainty about finding food in Egypt has been changed by Joseph's words, ***God has made me lord of all Egypt!*** Suddenly Jacob's pessimism is changed to ***"I will go and see him before I die!"*** But Jacob remembers his dealings with God, the God of his fathers over the years of his life. He is not without caution as he and his family load their wagons, corral their livestock and leave on the long journey.

READ GENESIS 46:1-7; 28-34

1. What is Jacob looking for when he stops over in Beersheba?

2. What is the significance of the way God identifies himself when he speaks to Jacob?

3. What promises does God make to reassure Jacob?

   Why might the decision to leave Canaan be a frightening one? Compare Genesis 26:2.

4. Jacob's guidance differs from that given Isaac. What does this teach you about the differing guidance God gives his people in different circumstances?

Note: It is no small thing for Jacob to be the one to take his family into **a country not their own** *(Genesis 15:13). Beersheba was a significant place in the history of both Abraham and Isaac, but the promise that God would go into Egypt with Jacob tells him that God is not tied to one locality.*

5. Quickly scan the listing of Jacob's family in verses 8-27. What do you notice about the arrangement of families, the death of grandchildren, the size of Benjamin's family, the number arriving in Egypt?

6. Jacob sends Judah ahead to alert Joseph of their arrival. What events of the past are swept away by the crowning moment of Jacob's reunion with Joseph?

7. What examples from your own experience are like the forgiveness experienced by this family?

8. Locate Goshen on a Bible map. What advantages does the location of Goshen offer Jacob's family and their flocks for the present and for the future (45:10)?

READ GENESIS 47:1-12

9. How does Joseph arrange for Pharaoh's approval of the plan to locate the family in Goshen?

10. When presented before the Pharaoh of Egypt, how does Jacob, the aged patriarch, act (verse 7-10)?

READ GENESIS 47:13-31

11. As the years of the famine lengthen, how does Joseph adjust his economic policy (verses 13-26)?

12. Verse 27 marks the first time the name ***Israelites*** refers to the whole family of Jacob. How have the Israelites fared in the seventeen years they have lived in Goshen?

13. Review God's promise to Jacob when he fled from home and saw the angels of God ascending and descending on the ladder to heaven (Genesis 28:13-15). What has Jacob seen of the fulfillment of these promises?

14. What reminder does Jacob give his family as he makes his burial plans known to Joseph?

How conscious do you think Jacob is in his old age of God's sovereign purposes for his family and their descendants?

15. What reminders are appropriate for you to give your own children or family members about God's purposes for their lives?

PSALM 28:6-9

16. What truths from this psalm has Joseph learned?

17. In what ways is verse 9 an appropriate prayer for Jacob as he prepares to die?

18. How would you phrase a prayer for your own family based on the verbs of verse 9: ***save, bless, be (their shepherd), carry***?

SUMMARY

1. Our world is full of refugees looking for food and safety. What is the difference between their experience and that of Jacob?

2. How can you sharpen your own sense that God has a long-range plan for you and your family, a destiny for his glory?

PRAYER

O Sovereign Lord, the lessons of this study are powerful and pertinent to our own lives. Help us to be so aware of your working in our lives that forgiveness is part of our daily experience.

Thank you that in Jesus Christ you have shown us what it means to be forgiven and loved unconditionally. Now give us new awareness of how you make the events of our lives work for our good and your glory so that we might praise you more willingly and gladly. Thank you for our time together, and for what you have taught us in this study. Amen.

DISCUSSION 13

The Blessing of Jacob

GENESIS 48—50; PSALM 66:8-20

Jacob is now one hundred and forty-seven years old. He is in Egypt, not Canaan, by God's design. He is more conscious than ever of *the God of his fathers.* His burial instructions remind his offspring that Egypt is not their home. Jacob gives a blessing and a prediction for each of his children. These blessings are unique in biblical history, but this is a unique family. No other family has been given a charge that would result in blessing the whole world. This family is part of God's plan for the salvation of the world.

READ GENESIS 48

1. What about his own past is Jacob remembering as he greets Joseph in verses 3 and 4? See 27:42-44 and 28:10-19.

2. In calling for Joseph to come to his bedside, what does Jacob intend to do (verse 5), and how will this affect Joseph's place in the family?

3. What clue does Jacob give in verse 7 for his reason for doing this?

4. Who is Jacob's firstborn and why does he not receive the blessing? Compare 49:3, 4, with 1 Chronicles 5:1, 2.

5. How does Jacob's quiet reversal of the blessings to Ephraim and Manasseh improve on his own personal history?

6. In what three ways does Jacob describe God in the course of invoking his blessing in verses 15, 16?

What would the names of Ephraim and Manasseh come to mean in the days ahead (verse 20)?

Note: Historically the blessing proved true. The tribes of Ephraim and Manasseh became particularly numerous and were given the largest tracts and most fertile lands when the Israelites entered Canaan.

READ GENESIS 49:1-28

Jacob's poetic words indicate that THE blessing has already been given. As you read, notice that some are rebukes for past actions, others are predictive. In the middle of his gloomy remarks, Jacob reaffirms his confidence in the LORD'S deliverance (verse 18).

7. What promise and prediction does Jacob give to Judah (verses 8-12)?

Jacob predicted more than he may have understood. What evidence do you see that ***the scepter*** is the Messiah who will come (verse 10)?

8. Although Jacob has already given the blessing to Ephraim and Manasseh, how does he show his obvious feelings for Joseph (verses 48:11 and 49:22-26)?

To what event in Joseph's youth do verses 23, 24 refer, and to whom does Jacob credit his deliverance?

9. Put the comment Jacob makes about his youngest son, Benjamin, in your own words.

Note: The tribe of Benjamin was known for its fierce fighting qualities. Benjamin led the tribes to battle under Deborah and Barak (Judges 5:14), and Psalm 68:27(NRSV) proclaims: ***There is Benjamin, the least of them, in the lead.***

READ GENESIS 49:29-32; 50:1-26

10. How do Jacob's instructions regarding his burial show his faith about the future?

11. What message does the enormous funeral procession that returns Jacob's body to Canaan give to everyone involved?

12. Back in Egypt, life is different without their father Jacob's presence. Why do you think Joseph weeps when he hears what his brothers are thinking in verses 15-18?

What makes it possible for you to forgive and to keep on doing good as Joseph did?

13. Later, how does Joseph on his deathbed demonstrate his unshakable confidence in God?

Note: Exodus 13:19 indicates that the descendants of Israel remembered Joseph's request.

PSALM 66:8-12; 16-20

14. How does what God does for a community (verses 8-12) relate to what he does in someone's personal life (verses 16-20)?

Apply these verses to Joseph's life.

15. How can your own experience with God affect the life of your community (family)?

SUMMARY

1. What actions does Hebrews 11:21, 22 single out to illustrate the faith of Jacob and the faith of Joseph?

   Why did these actions require faith?

2. What qualities in Joseph make him an exemplary model for your own life?

Prayer

Dear Lord, we have followed the turbulent history of Jacob's life and marveled at your grace to him as his Shepherd, his Rock, the Almighty God, his Deliverer. We see your sovereign hand at every turn in his life. Thank you, too, for the faith of Joseph and the way you used him to save your people. Keep us trusting you, full of confidence that your hand is on our personal lives to bring about whatever you purpose for us. We conclude this study with praise for all we have learned about you, for our good and your glory. Amen.

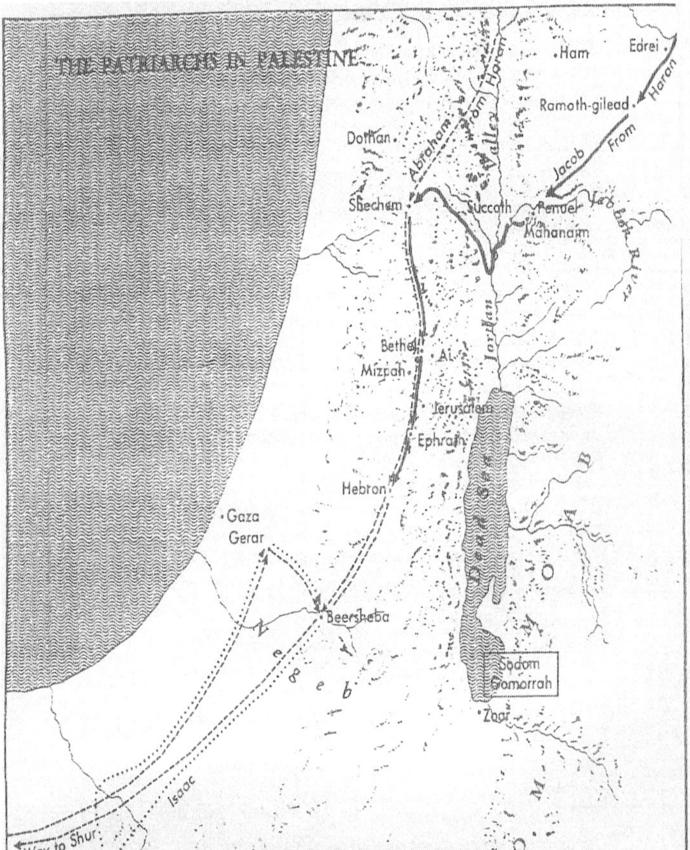
THE PATRIARCHS IN PALESTINE
Ham
Edrei
Haran
Ramoth-gilead
From
Jacob
Dothan
Abraham
Shechem
Succoth
Penuel
Mahanaim
Jordan
Bethel
Ai
Mizpah
Jerusalem
Ephrath
Dead Sea
Hebron
Gaza
Gerar
Beersheba
Negeb
Sodom
Gomorrah
Zoar
Isaac
Way to Shur
Kadesh-barnea
Wilderness of Paran
0 10 20 miles
0 10 20 30 km.

WHAT SHOULD OUR GROUP STUDY NEXT?

We recommend the Gospel of Mark, the fast paced narrative of Jesus' life, as the first book for people new to Bible study. Follow this with the Book of Acts to see what happens to the people introduced in Mark. Then in Genesis discover the beginnings of the world and find the answers to the big questions of where we came from and why we are here.

Our repertoire of guides allows great flexibility. For groups starting with *Lenten Studies*, *They Met Jesus* is a good sequel.

LEVEL 101: little or no previous Bible study experience

Mark *(recommended first unit of study) or* The Book of Mark *(Simplified English)*
Acts, Books 1 and 2
Genesis, Books 1 and 2
Psalms/Proverbs
Topical Studies
Conversations With Jesus
Lenten Studies
Foundations for Faith
Character Studies
They Met Jesus

Sequence for groups reaching people from non-Christian cultures
Foundations for Faith
Genesis, Books 1 and 2
Mark, Discover Jesus *or*
The Book of Mark
(Simplified English)

LEVEL 201: some experience in Bible study (after 3-4 Level 101 books)

John, Books 1 and 2
Romans
I John/James
1 Corinthians
2 Corinthians
Philippians
Colossians
Topical Studies
Prayer
Treasures
Relationships
Servants of the Lord
Change
Work – God's Gift
Celebrate
Character Studies
Four Men of God
Lifestyles of Faith, Books 1 and 2

LEVEL 301: More experienced in Bible study

Matthew, Books 1 and 2
Galatians & Philemon
1 and 2 Peter
Hebrews
1 and 2 Thessalonians, 2 & 3 John
Isaiah
Ephesians
Topical Studies
Set Free
Character Studies
David
Moses

***Biweekly or Monthly Groups may use topical studies or character studies.*

ABOUT NEIGHBORHOOD BIBLE STUDIES

Neighborhood Bible Studies, Inc. is a leader in the field of small group Bible studies. Since 1960, NBS has pioneered the development of Bible study groups that encourage each member to participate in the leadership of the discussion.

The Mission of Neighborhood Bible Studies is to mobilize Christians to facilitate group discussions with spiritual seekers so they can find God as revealed in the Bible.

The Vision of Neighborhood Bible Studies is for Christians all over the world inviting people into small groups to question, discover and grow in their relationship with God.

Publication in more than 20 languages indicates the versatility of NBS cross culturally. NBS **methods and materials** are used around the world to:

Equip individuals for facilitating discovery Bible studies
Serve as a resource to the church

Skilled NBS personnel provide consultation by telephone or e-mail. In some areas, they conduct workshops and seminars to train individuals, clergy, and laity in how to establish small group Bible studies in neighborhoods, churches, workplaces and specialized facilities. **Call 1-800-369-0307 to inquire about consultation or training.**

ABOUT THE FOUNDERS

Marilyn Kunz and Catherine Schell, authors of many of the NBS guides, founded Neighborhood Bible Studies and directed its work for thirty-one years. Currently other authors contribute to the series.

The cost of your study guide has been subsidized by faithful people who give generously to NBS. For more information, visit our web site: www.neighborhoodbiblestudy.org ***1-800-369-0307***

About the Author

Gladys M. Hunt is enthusiastic about the value of small group discussion Bible studies. Since her college days and her involvement in InterVarsity Christian Fellowship she has been a catalyst and a participant in outreach discussion groups, believing that "truth personally discovered for one's self" is life-changing. She is the author of numerous Bible study guides and has done revision work for Neighborhood Bible Studies. Married to Keith Hunt, she is also a mother and grandmother, and enjoys sharing the opportunities offered by the two places she lives: the university community of Ann Arbor, Michigan and her outdoor life on the shores of Lake Huron.

Complete Listing of NBS Study Guides

Getting Started

How to Start a Q Place

Bible Book Studies

Genesis, Book 1 *Begin with God*
Genesis, Book 2 *Discover Your Roots*
Psalms & Proverbs *Journals of Wisdom*
Isaiah *God's Help Is on the Way*
Matthew, Book 1 *God's Promise Kept*
Matthew, Book 2 *God's Purpose Fulfilled*
Mark *Discover Jesus*
Luke *Good News and Great Joy*
John, Book 1 *Explore Faith and Understand Life*
John, Book 2 *Believe and Live*
Acts, Book 1 *The Holy Spirit Transforms Lives*
Acts, Book 2 *Amazing Journeys with God*
Romans *A Reasoned Faith*
1 Corinthians *Finding Answers to Life's Questions*
2 Corinthians *The Power of Weakness*
Galatians & Philemon *Fully Accepted by God*
Ephesians *Living in God's Family*
Philippians *A Message of Encouragement*
Colossians *Staying Focused on Truth*
1 & 2 Thessalonians, 2 & 3 John, Jude *The Coming of the LORD*
Hebrews *Access to God*
1 & 2 Peter *Strength Amidst Stress*
1 John & James *Faith that Lives*

Topical Studies

Celebrate *Reasons for Hurrahs*
Conversations with Jesus *Getting to Know Him*
Change *Facing the Unexpected*
Foundations for Faith *The Basics for Knowing God*
Lenten Studies *Life Defeats Death*
Prayer *Communicating with God*
Relationships *Connect to Others: God's Plan*
Servants of the LORD *Embrace God's Agenda*
Set Free *Leaving Negative Emotions Behind*
Treasures *Discover God's Riches*
Work - God's Gift *Life-Changing Choices*

Character Studies

Four Men of God *Unlikely Leaders*
Lifestyles of Faith, Book One *Choosing to Trust God*
Lifestyles of Faith, Book Two *Choosing to Obey God*
They Met Jesus *Life-Changing Encounters*
David *Passions Pursued*
Moses *Learning to Lead*

Simplified English

The Book of Mark *The Story of Jesus*